A PRACTICAL MANUAL
FOR EMOTIONAL SURVIVAL

This remarkable book deals in a warm, informative and directly helpful way with one of the most common (and certainly most painful) of human experiences—loss.

Written by a psychologist, a psychiatrist and a poet, this kindly, witty and companionable book is a unique guide to overcoming grief and unhappiness—a practical manual for emotional survival.

Divided into fifty-eight sections, *HOW TO SURVIVE THE LOSS OF A LOVE* offers a gathering of things the reader can *do*, things that comfort and help in a real and natural way.

"One of the loveliest books ever written . . . It should be in everybody's library."

—Merv Griffin

How to Survive the Loss of a Love

58 things to do when there is nothing to be done

Melba Colgrove, Ph.D.,
Harold H.
Bloomfield, M.D.
& Peter A. McWilliams

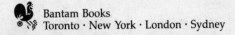
Bantam Books
Toronto · New York · London · Sydney

HOW TO SURVIVE THE LOSS OF A LOVE

*A Bantam Book / published by arrangement with
Prelude Press*

PRINTING HISTORY

Leo Press hardcover edition published March 1976

*Bantam rack-size edition / February 1977
11 printings through September 1981*

*Bantam trade edition / March 1983
6 printings through February 1988*

The poetry in this book is taken from Peter McWilliams' already published collections, which include: Come Love With Me and Be My Life / For Lovers and No Others / I Love Therefore I Am / The Hard Stuff: Love / Love and All the Other Verbs of Life / Love . . . An Experience of / Love is Yes. Published by Prelude Press, 5806 Elizabeth Court, Allen Park, Michigan 48101.

ISBN 0-553-01481-1

Library of Congress Catalog Card No.: 82-45944

Published simultaneously in the United States and Canada

Bantam Books are published by Bantam Books, a division of Bantam Doubleday Dell Publishing Group, Inc. Its trademark, consisting of the words "Bantam Books" and the portrayal of a rooster, is Registered in U.S. Patent and Trademark Office and in other countries. Marca Registrada. Bantam Books, 666 Fifth Avenue, New York, New York 10103.

PRINTED IN THE UNITED STATES OF AMERICA

CW   15   14   13   12   11   10   9   8

DEDICATION

To All Good.
To my Father, whose death when I was four,
    constituted a near overwhelming loss.
To my Mother, Grandparents, and all those perceptive
        others—then and now—who help
        me to survive, heal and grow.
To Jim Seppala, Sam and Nancy Manser, N.R.F. Maier,
        Mary Katherine MacDougall, Catherine Knight
        and

To all those who refuse for long to remain
        deadened, indifferent or uncaring
        . . . choosing instead to come alive again.
                                            Melba

Dedicated to my Parents, Sister and Family for their love and support . . . To Andi, to Susan—for their love, our shared loss and the growth . . . To my patients . . . to the wonder and joy of it all.

To Maharishi Mahesh Yogi, who brought the Transcendental Meditation program into my life at a time when I needed it most.

                                            Harold

For Melba & Joan & Ginny, for Mom, and for all who helped me survive,
                        Thank you!
                                            Peter

Our mutual thanks and appreciation to Bev Nichols, Michael Korda, Carlo DiGovanna, John Russ, Melba Swick, Jane O'Wyatt, Cecilia Hunt, Brad Miner and Charles Addams.

AUTHORS' NOTES

How to Survive the Loss of a Love is a book to be *used*, not just read.

This book will help define loss, as not all loss is either obvious or immediate. It will then offer guidelines to facilitate survival, encourage healing and maximize growth. Certainly, anything the reader has found personally helpful in overcoming past losses should be reutilized at this time.

We would like to state at the outset that this book is not designed to be a definitive text. Neither is it presented as a substitute for therapy. If you feel the need, see your doctor. Your general hospital emergency room is available twenty-four hours a day. Help of all sorts can be found in, of all places, the Yellow Pages, under "Social Services" or "Welfare Organizations."

You should seek professional help *at once* if you:

- feel suicidal
- feel you are "coming apart"
- are no longer in control
- have a history of severe emotional disturbance
- turn to alcohol or drugs in time of stress
- are isolated with no one to turn to
- repeatedly find yourself in "loss situations"

When an emotional injury has taken place, the body begins a process as natural as the healing of a physical wound. Let the process happen. Trust that nature will do the healing. Know that the pain will pass and, when it passes, you will be stronger, happier, more sensitive and aware.

The fact that you are reading these pages means that you have already chosen to survive. Congratulations, and welcome.

CONTENTS

thirty-seven: you're stronger now / *thirty-eight:* forgive the other person / *thirty-nine:* forgive yourself / *forty:* take stock of the good / *forty-one:* you are a better person for having loved / *forty-two:* changes / *forty-three:* praise yourself for the courage to relate / *forty-four:* start anew / *forty-five:* invite new people into your life / *forty-six:* develop new interests / *forty-seven:* . . . but don't forget the old interests / *forty-eight:* groups / *forty-nine:* self-improvement anyone? / *fifty:* do something for someone else / *fifty-one:* the past / *fifty-two:* solitude / *fifty-three:* creativity / *fifty-four:* appreciation / *fifty-five:* growth / *fifty-six:* freedom to choose / *fifty-seven:* celebrate your survival / *fifty-eight:* a pat on the back for a job well done.

THE LOSS

I find.
I lost.

Let's take a moment to view loss in a large perspective. In nature, loss is an essential element of creation: the rose blossoms, the bud is lost; the plant sprouts, the seed is lost; the day begins, the night is lost. In all cases, loss sets the stage for further creation (or, more properly, re-creation).

So it is in human life. Our baby teeth are lost and our permanent teeth take root. Our permanent teeth are lost and an understanding of the Poly-Grip ads is gained. Sometimes the feeling of loss can even come after a gain, but more often the loss precedes it. It's hard to look back upon any gain in life that does not have a loss attached to it.

With this firmly in mind we can examine the various losses in life. (Without this overview it tends to become awfully depressing.)

OBVIOUS LOSSES

—death of a loved one
—the break-up of an affair
—separation
—divorce

NOT SO OBVIOUS LOSSES

—loss of job
—loss of money
—moving
—illness (loss of health)
—changing teachers, changing schools
—robbery
—success (the loss of striving)
—loss of a cherished ideal
—loss of a long-term goal

LOSSES RELATED TO AGE

—childhood dreams
—puppy love
—crushes
—adolescent romances
—leaving school (dropping out or graduation)
—leaving home
—change of jobs
—loss of "youth"
—loss of "beauty"
—loss of hair and/or teeth
—loss of sexual drive (or worse, the drive remains but the ability falters)
—menopause
—retirement

LIMBO

(Is it on? Is it off? Is it a gain? Is it a loss?)

—awaiting medical tests or reports on their outcome
—a couple on the brink of divorce for the fourteenth time
—a friend, spouse or relative "missing in action"
—lovers, after any quarrel
—a business transaction that may or may not fall through

Limbo losses often feel like this:

my life has fallen down
around me before—
lots of times—
for lots of reasons—
usually other people.

and most of the time
I was fortunate enough
to have a large lump of
that life hit me on the
head and render me numb
to the pain & desolation
that followed.
and I survived.
and I lived to Love again.

But This,
this slow erosion from below
—or within—
It's me falling down around my life
because you're still in that life
—but not really.
and you're out of that life
—but not quite

I do alright
alone
and better
together
but
I do very poorly
when
semi-
together.

in solitude
I do much
in love
I do more
but
in doubt
I only transfer
pain to paper
in gigantic Passion Plays
complete with miracles and martyrs
and crucifixions and resurrections.

come to stay
or
stay away.

this series of passion poems
is becoming a heavy cross to bare.

It is important to note that the feeling of being "in limbo" is in itself a loss. Even if the situation turns out fine (the veteran returns, the lover calls and again professes undying love, etc.) while in doubt, that doubt is a loss and should be dealt with accordingly.

- Realize that "not knowing" may be the worst torture of all.

- When in limbo, and your better instincts tell you there's little hope, it's better to end the situation than to let it drag on and on.

- Call or send in your formal notice of termination and get on with the business of surviving /healing/ growing.

to give you up.

God!
what a bell of freedom
that rings within me

no more waiting for
letters
phone calls
post cards
that never come.

no more creative energy
wasted
in letters never mailed.

and, after awhile,

no more insomnia.
no more insanity.

some more happiness.
some more life.

all it took was giving you up.

and that took quite a bit.

INEVITABLE LOSSES

There are inevitable losses . . . losses in which death or separation is imminent. When you recognize these in advance it will help greatly to:

- discuss your situation with the person who is leaving
- if you are the one who is leaving, talk it over with those who are being left
- share in making the decisions that must be made
- let your wishes be known

OTHER LOSSES

Temporary losses (lover on vacation, spouse in the service, son or daughter away at school, a slump in business), even though we know the outcome will eventually be positive, are losses nonetheless.

Even success has built into it certain losses—the loss of a goal to strive for: after the Cadillac or the Continental, what? (Well, the obvious answer is a Mercedes, but after the Mercedes, what?) (We know, a Porsche—but you get the idea.)

There are also the innumerable "mini losses" that tend to add up during the course of a day, week, month or life. An unexpected dent in the car here, an argument with a friend there, and one soon finds oneself "inexplicably" depressed.

Each of these losses, immediate or cumulative, sudden or eventual, obvious or not, creates an emotional wound, an injury to the organism.

WHAT LOSS FEELS LIKE

This chapter may appear to be carrying the proverbial coals to Newcastle; after all, everyone knows what loss feels like, right? Well, not necessarily. Along with the obvious feelings of pain, depression and sadness there are other reactions to loss that are not so obvious, such as:

- feeling helpless, fearful, empty, despairing, pessimistic, irritable, angry, guilty, restless.
- experiencing a loss of concentration, hope, motivation, energy.
- any changes in appetite, sleep patterns, or sexual drive.
- a tendency to be more fatigued, error-prone, and slower in speech and movement.

Any or all of these are to be expected during and after the experience of a loss. It's part of the body's natural healing process. Be with these changes; don't fight them. It's OK.

If you relate strongly to a good number of these reactions, you may want to examine the recent past to see if a not-so-obvious loss has taken place in your life. If so, you might want to follow a few of the suggestions given, remaining aware that your mind and body are already involved in the healing process.

THE STAGES OF RECOVERY

Following a loss there are three recognizable stages of recovery

The first is **shock/denial**

> *morning.*
> *we wake & snuggle.*
>
> *after noon.*
> *a phone call, california beckons.*
>
> *evening.*
> *the air port, a brutal good(?) bye.*
>
> *night.*
> *o my god. o my god. o my god.*
>
> *mourning. again.*

> *You're going?*
> *oh?*
> *for how long?*
> *oh.*
> *where are you going?*
> *oh*
> *I'm going someplace too!*
> *oh,*
> *insane.*

the fear that I would
come home one day and
find you gone has turned
into the pain of the
reality.

"What will I do if it happens?"
I would ask myself.

What will I do
now that it
has?

I know it was time for us
to part,

      but today?

I know I had much pain to
go through,

      but tonight

       ?

The next, **anger/depression**

rain,
it
rained.
I
fell.
it
rained.
I
loved.
it
rained
I lost.
it
rained.
It loved.
I rained.
rain.

as the memory of your
light fades
my days grow dark.

my nights are lit with
electric bulbs. I cannot
sleep. I am afraid of the
dark. I am afraid that you
will return and then fade
again. I am afraid that you
will never return. I am
afraid that my next thought
will be of you. I am afraid
that I will run out of poems
before I run out of pain.

What do I do
now that you're gone?

well, when there's
nothing else going on,
which is quite often,
I sit in a corner and
I cry
until I am
too numbed
to feel.

Paralyzed motionless
for awhile, nothing
moving
inside or out.

then I think
how much I miss you.

then I feel
fear
pain
loneliness
desolation.

then
I cry
until I am
too numbed
to feel

interesting pastime.

and finally, **understanding/acceptance**

the sun will rise
in a few minutes

it's been doing it
—regularly—
for as long as I
can remember.

maybe I should
pin my hopes
on important,
but often
unnoticed,
certainties
like that,

not on such relatively
trivial matters as
whether you will ever
love me or not.

I must conquer my loneliness

alone.

I must be happy with myself
or I have
nothing
to offer.

Two halves have
little choice
but to
join;
and yes,
they do
make a
whole.

but two
wholes
when they coincide . . .

that is
beauty.

that is
love.

It's good to be aware of these phases of recovery and to know that each is both necessary and natural. The progression is from shock/denial to anger/depression and finally to understanding/acceptance.

It is important to note that the body goes through these same three phases of recovery no matter how tragic or how seemingly trivial a loss might be. The only difference is the *length of time* it takes to go through the three phases and the *intensity* of emotion felt during each.

A major loss, such as the death of a spouse, might take several years to heal. The body might be numbed, literally "in shock," for as long as six months. It is very common for someone to comment during this time, "I still can't believe he/she is gone." This is a form of the denial phase. The anger/depression phase of a major loss may take two years, and sometimes longer, before the individual can truly come to a point of understanding and acceptance.

On the other hand, after a minor loss the three stages of recovery can be fully experienced in as little as ten seconds, for example the case of a lost phone call: we run to a ringing phone and just as we pick it up, the caller hangs up. Our first thought might be, "Oh no. I couldn't have missed it!" (shock/denial). Our next thought, "Why didn't they hold on a little longer?" or "Why didn't I get here sooner?" (anger, which can be expressed against the other person, ourselves, or more often both). Then: "Gee, I really wanted to talk with somebody," (depression). And finally: "Oh well, if it was important they'll call back," (understanding/acceptance), and we return to what we were doing, or call another friend, or order an extension phone, or buy an answering machine, depending on how we individually deal with the aftermath of loss. The whole process might take place in a few seconds, but the three stages of recovery have been experienced, the body has healed, and we are ready to continue with life.

SURVIVING

thursday: *drowning in love*

friday: *drowning in doubt*

saturday: *drowning.*

sunday: *God, I can't drag my
self to church this morning.
please make a house call.*

One:
Recognize the Loss

- You can expect to be in shock for a while. This emotional numbness may be frightening.

- You may struggle both to believe and to disbelieve that this could have happened to you.

- It has happened. It is real.

- Recognize that a loss has taken place.

- You may wonder if you are strong enough to bear such a loss.

- You are strong enough.

- You will survive.

it is as though you were
    dead.

there is nothing to be
    done.

only accept it . . .

and hurt.

Two:
Be with the Pain

- You're hurting. Admit it.

- To feel pain after a loss is:
    —normal
    —proof that you are alive
    —a sign that you are able to respond to life's experiences.

- Although you may find yourself frightened by it, be with your pain. Feel it. Lean into it. You will not find it bottomless.

- It is important to the healing process that you be with the pain, experience the desolation, feel the hurt.

- Don't deny it or cover it or run away from it. Be with it. Hurt for a while.

pain
>
> is not so heavy
> a burden in the
> summer.

walks
>
> through
> travelogue scenes
> prevent a good
> deal of destruction.

and
>
> even though no one
> is there to warm me,
> the sun will.

but
>
> Fall just fell
> leaving Winter,
> and me
> with no warmth
> within to face
> the cold without.

I might just stick
to the sidewalk
and freeze.

Three:
You Are Not Alone

- Loss is a part of life—of being alive—of being human.

- Everyone experiences loss.

- Your task is to make the journey from immediate loss to eventual gain as rapidly, smoothly, and comfortably as possible.

- Somehow the camaraderie of mutual suffering eases the pain. You have comrades.

I hope I heal soon.

I want to enjoy
        autumn.

Four:
You're Great!

- You are a good, whole, worthwhile human being.

- You are OK. You're more than OK, you're *great*.

- Your self-esteem may have suffered a jolt, and your thoughts may be full of guilt, worry, condemnation and self-deprecation. These thoughts are just symptoms of the stress you are going through.

- There is no need to give negative thoughts about yourself prime-time status.

- Don't punish yourself with "if only's" (*if only* I had [or hadn't] done this or that I wouldn't be in this emotional rat-trap). Disregard any thought that begins "if only."

- You are much more than the emotional wound you are currently suffering. Don't lose sight of that.

- Beneath the surface turmoil
    —you are good
    —you are whole
    —you are beautiful
    just because you are.

I sat evaluating
myself.

I decided
to lie down.

Five:
You Will Survive

- You *will* get better.

- No doubt about it.

- It is the nature of the healing process to have a beginning, a middle and an end.

- Keep in mind, at the beginning, that there *is* an end. It's not that far off. You *will* heal.

- Nature is on your side, and nature is a powerful ally.

*I found
in you
a home.*

*Your departure
left me a
Shelterless Victim
of a
Major Disaster*

*I called the
Red Cross
but they
refused to
send over
a nurse.*

Six:
Give Yourself Time to Heal

- The healing process takes time.

- The greater the loss, the more time it will take to heal.

- It's hard to accept the fact that anything takes time in this age of fast foods and instantly replaceable everything.

- In the speed and immediacy of modern life, we are not accustomed to giving ourselves time.

- You require time to heal. Give yourself the luxury. You deserve it.

- The healing will happen. (It's happening right now!)

I shall miss loving you.

I shall miss the
Comfort
of your embrace.

I shall miss the
Loneliness
of waiting for your
calls that never came.

I shall miss the Joy
of our comings,
and Pain
of your goings.

and,
after a time,
I shall miss

missing
loving
you.

Seven:
The Healing Process Has Its Progressions and Regressions

- The process of healing and growth is not the smooth progression many people assume:

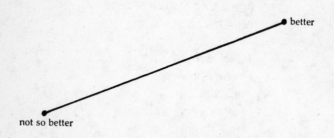

- It's more a lightning bolt, full of ups and down, progressions and regressions, dramatic leaps and depressing backslides.

- Realize this and know that the healing process is under way.

life is becoming.
less livable.

with each new person I meet
I wonder, is this the day
fate has chosen, or is fate
what I have chosen to get me
through the day.

loving
is the most
creative
force of the universe.

the memory of loving
the most
destructive.

Eight:
Tomorrow Will Come

- Remember that life is full of positive experiences, and that the positive is on its way.

- Tomorrow will come.

- We should look for a moment at the words of that great thinker, prophet and philosopher, Scarlett O'Hara. You will recall that Scarlett has been abandoned by Rhett on the red velvet staircase of their Atlanta mansion. Rhett has professed that he frankly doesn't give a damn, and Scarlett, furrowed with tears, proclaims, "I'll think about it tomorrow at Tara. After all, tomorrow is another day!"

The authors of this volume would like to respectfully disagree with Ms. O'Hara (or, more correctly, Ms. Butler) on the first point. It would be far better not to postpone the grieving until "tomorrow at Tara." However, the nugget of wisdom we would like to illuminate is the "Tomorrow is another day" aspect. After all, tomorrow *is* another day. It *will* come and you *will* heal.

first
I have to get
out
of love with you.

second
I have to remember

don't fall
until you see
the whites
of their
lies

Nine:
Get Lots of Rest—Now

• Rest

• Sleep more.

• Obtain help with ongoing tasks.

• Arrange your life so that you get lots of rest. Schedule rest into the day. *Plan* to go to bed earlier and sleep a bit later.

• Go gently. Don't rush around too much. Your body needs energy for repair.

• Meditate.

• Rest your emotions. Don't become "heavily involved" for awhile.

• Productive work often helps rest the emotions. Do as much of that as is comfortable.

• Rest is the guardian of health.

(there is no poem
on this page
as the poet
decided to
take a nap)

Ten:
Stick to Your Schedule

- Enough rest! Get yourself in gear!

- The most efficient healing takes place when sufficient rest and dynamic activity are alternated.

- Rest as much as you need, but don't become lethargic. Keep busy.

- While your internal world is chaotic, keep to a schedule in the outer. This will give a sense of order—also something to hold on to.

- A few days off for nothing but rest is fine, other than that, keep to a routine; go by your schedule.

although my
nature is not to
live by day

I can not
tolerate another
night like this.

so.

I will wake up
early
tomorrow morning and
do do do
all day long,

falling asleep
exhausted tomorrow
early evening,
too tired
even for
nightmares.

Eleven:
Keep Decision-Making to a Minimum

- Expect your judgment to be clouded these days, therefore,
    - —keep decision-making to a minimum
    - —postpone major decisions if at all possible
    - —friends and family can make many minor decisions for you; invite them to do so

- Enough change has taken place already—that's why you're hurting. Keep additional change to a minimum for awhile. Think twice (at least) before making any major changes, take a hot bath, and think again.

- But then, some people thrive on change and grow faster during change. You'll soon find out which mode you prefer.

Plans:
next month:

       find someone new.

this month:

       get over you.

this week:

       get you back.

today:

       survive.

Twelve:
It's OK to Need Comforting

- It's OK to be taken care of for awhile.

- Accept understanding and support from:
    —friends
    —family
    —co-workers

- An emotional wound is real, disabling and painful. It's OK to need comfort.

- Some people are so good at comforting that they do it professionally. Feel free to seek the help of a mental health professional with whom you feel comfortable.

- Be brave enough to accept the help of others.

My friends are still there:

neglected,
rejected
while I gave all my
precious moments to
you.

they're still here!

god bless them.

Thirteen:
Seek the Support of Others

- Don't be afraid to ask for help. It's a human (and courageous) thing to do.

- Mobilize your friends and family into a *support system*. You need to know that others care and, if they know your pain, they will help.

- The telephone is a marvelous tool of communication. Use it. Call a friend, a "rap line," or a professional. (Again, check the Yellow Pages under "Social Services" or "Welfare Organizations." As corny as those classifications sound, remember you are in *need* of a little social service and a bit of welfare right now!)

- Invite a friend to stay overnight.

- Visit a relative (preferably at dinnertime!).

- Don't forget that neighbors can be wonderful.

help me up
my friend.

dust me off.

feed me warmth.

you are comfort.

let me lean on you
until I can stand
      alone.

I will then stand a little taller.

and you will be
proud
to have a friend
such as I.

Fourteen:
Surround Yourself with Things that Are Alive

• Don't isolate yourself from life.

• In addition to friends and family, bring other living
  things into your life-space these days:
  —a new plant
  —a stray kitty
  —the puppy you've always wanted
  —a brandy snifter of goldfish
  —even a bowl of fresh fruit has its own joy and
    consolation to offer

I'd have a nervous breakdown
only
I've been through
this too many
times to be
nervous

Fifteen:
Re-affirm Your Beliefs

- Re-affirm any beliefs in which you have faith.

- They may include religious beliefs or philosophical concepts in which you put stock.

- Use any body of knowledge which you find comforting: re-explore it, lean on it, grow from it, enjoy it.

missing your love
with God's so
close at hand.

It seems somehow
a sacrilege . . .

but I think
He understands.

Sixteen:
Sundays Are the Worst!

- No doubt about it.

- Holidays are the second worst.

- Saturday nights aren't much fun, either.

- Schedule activities that you find particularly comforting into these periods of time.

Yesterday was Sunday
Sundays are always bad
("bloody," as they have been aptly described).

The full moon is Wednesday.
Full moons are always bad.
(ask Lon Chaney).

Friday is Good Friday
and, 30 miles from Rome,
the vibrations of all those mourning
Italians will make it bad.

Sunday is Easter—but it's also
Sunday,
        and Sundays are always bad.

Seventeen:
The Question of Suicide

- You may be having suicidal thoughts. They may not be as eloquent as *"To be or not to be,"* but they may arise.

- Know they are a natural symptom of the pain and that there is no need to act on them.

- If you are afraid these impulses are getting out of hand, seek professional help *at once*. Call the operator and ask her to connect you with the local suicide prevention agency. He or she may ask (as Ma Bell has instructed them) "Is this an emergency?" Answer with a resounding "Yes!"

- Don't turn the rage you feel against yourself (although feeling rage is perfectly all right—after all, an utterly outrageous thing has happened to you). Find a safe way to let the rage out. Beat a pillow, cry, scream, stomp up and down, yell.

- Above all, suicide is dumb. It's leaving the world series ten minutes into the first inning just because your favorite hitter struck out. It's walking out of the opera during the overture just because the conductor dropped his baton. It's . . . well, you get the picture.

- The feeling *will pass*. You can count on that. You *will* get better. *Much* better.

- We *do* promise you a rose garden. We just can't promise that it will be totally without thorns.

THE QUESTION OF SUICIDE:

Keep it a question.
  It's not really an answer

HEALING

one thing I forgot:

after the
pain of parting
comes the
happiness of healing.

rediscovering
    life,
    friends,
    self.

Joy.

Eighteen:
Do Your Mourning Now

• Don't postpone or deny or cover, or run away from your pain. Be with that pain. **NOW.**

• Everything else can wait. An emotional wound requires the same priority attention as a physical wound. Set time aside for mourning.

• The sooner you allow yourself to be with your pain, the sooner it will pass.

• If you resist the mourning, you will be interfering with the body's natural stages of repair.

• If you postpone the healing process, grief can return months or even years later to haunt you.

Grief is a quiet thing
Deadly in repose.
A raging horror, a thunder of abuse

Raucous—
Demanding—
Incomprehensible—
Tearing all that one has ever loved.

Hopeless,
Forlorn,
Fear-ridden and misunderstood;
Ceasing a moment, and through the years
Returning . . . to destroy.

To rage,
To curse all that is happy—
or contented,
or trusting.

To threaten every beauty that is true.

Grief?
It's a quiet thing.

—Melba Colgrove

Nineteen:
Be Gentle with Yourself

- Be *very* gentle with yourself.

- Accept the fact that you have an emotional wound, that it is disabling and that it will take awhile before you are completely well.

- So treat yourself with the same care and affection that you would offer a good friend in a similar situation.

- Don't take on many new responsibilities. When appropriate, let your co-workers and employer know you're healing.

- Avoid situations in which you might over react.

- Accept help and support when offered, but remember that care and compassion begin at home.

- Above all, don't blame yourself for any "mistakes" (real or imagined), you may have made that brought you to this situation of loss.

Twenty:
Let Yourself Heal Fully

• Let the healing process run its full course.

• A time of convalescence is very important.

• For a while don't become involved in an all-consuming passionate romance or a new project that requires great time and energy.

• Just follow your daily routine—and let yourself heal.

• If you do not allow the hurt to heal completely you may find emotional over-sensitivity the result. You might flinch at every new encounter. Let yourself heal.

Twenty-one:
Don't Try To Re-kindle the Old Relationship

- Futile attempts at "reconciliation" are
  —painful
  —anti-healing
  —anti-growth
  —a waste of valuable energy

- To give up this final hope may be the most difficult of all.

- Invest your energies in healing and growing, in new relationships and in life.

the layers I have put
around the pain of
your going are thin.

I walk softly through
life, adding thickness
each day.

a thought or a feeling
of you cracks the surface.

a call to you
shatters it all.

I spend that night in death

and spin the first
layer of life
with the sunrise.

Twenty-two:
Make a Pact with a Friend

- If the urge to call or contact the "long-lost love" is strong, make a pact—a contract—with a friend.

- Don't make the pact unreasonable. "I will never ever see him/her as long as I live!" is unreasonable.

- "I will not call him/her unless I call you first and talk it over" is reasonable.

She asked me if seeing
you was a drain.

Seeing you is not a drain.

It's a sewer.

Twenty-three:
Mementos

- If you find photographs and mementos helpful to the mourning process, use them.

- If you find mementos bind you to a dead past, get rid of them. (Put them in the attic, sell them, give them away, or throw them out.)

I ceremoniously disposed
of all the objects connected
with you. I thought they were
contaminated.
                    It did not help.

I'm *the one that's contaminated!*

Twenty-four:
Anticipate a Positive Outcome

- That to which we give our attention grows stronger in our lives.

- Expect a positive outcome. Anticipate it. Plan for it. It *will* come.

- Be with the sadness and the pain when it comes, but don't dwell on it. Accept it, but don't invite it. Pain is an acceptable guest, but not a welcome long-term visitor.

Twenty-five:
It's OK to Feel Depressed

- Pretending to have more energy or enthusiasm or happiness than you actually have is not productive.

- It's OK to be low-key for awhile.

- Crying has its own specialness. It is cleansing, a marvelous release.

Twenty-six:
It's OK to Feel Anger

- Everyone gets angry at the loss of love. Everyone.

- It's OK to feel your anger.

- It's OK to feel anger toward:
  —the person who left you (even if they left you through death)
  —the person who took something or someone away
  —the social conventions or customs that contributed to the loss
  —the fates

- It's *not* OK to:
  —hate yourself
  —act upon your anger in a destructive way

- Let the anger out (safely, please!):
  —hit a pillow
  —kick on a bed
  —yell and scream (when alone, with the windows closed. A car parked in a deserted place makes a great "scream-chamber.")
  —play volleyball, tennis, handball, soccer
  —hit a punching bag
  —play piano at full crescendo

- If the anger is channeled and dissipated in these harmless (indeed, helpful) ways, you'll avoid senseless arguments, accidents and ulcers.

- Your anger will go away as your hurt heals.

I'm past the point of going
  quietly insane.

I'm getting quite
  noisy about it.

The neighbors must think
  I'm mad.

The neighbors, for once,
  think right.

Twenty-seven:
Nutrition

• Now is not the time to alter your eating habits drastically or go on a crash diet. Good nutrition tends to speed the healing process.

• Increase the amount of protein you eat. Protein includes meat, fish, fowl, milk, eggs, nuts, seeds, soy beans, and whole grains.

• Decrease junk foods.

• Take a B-vitamin supplement, a C-vitamin supplement, and a multi-vitamin/mineral supplement. (Note: It's a good idea to buy vitamins at health food stores rather than drug stores. But while at the health food store, stay away from the wonder-cure books, unless you're in need of a laugh.)

• Increase calcium (take calcium tablets or better still, drink more milk) and potassium (again in tablets, or by eating baked potatoes, parsley or bananas).

• And, as they told you in eighth grade health class, eat something every day from each of the four major food groups: meat & poultry, dairy products, fruits & vegetables, breads & cereals.

Twenty-eight:
Remember: You're Vulnerable

- Remember in these days of stress and recovery that you are vulnerable.

- Guard your physical health
    —get rest
    —don't overextend
    —eat well
    —get moderate exercise

- Don't enter into situations or purchases that involve your being "convinced" of their merit. Your sales resistance will be low. Keep that in mind.

- Invite help from those who are
    —trustworthy
    —able to do what you request of them

- There is no need to overprotect yourself. Just be aware of the fact that a lot of your energy is being used for healing and that the body's natural defense systems may be weakened.

Twenty-nine:
Beware of the Rebound

- Nature abhors a vacuum, and you may find yourself rushing prematurely into romantic attachments in an attempt to fill that grinding emptiness.

- If your healing hasn't been completed, an initial rebound is likely to be followed quickly by another loss, a second rebound, another loss, and another, until your emotional life is being lived in the ricocheted pattern of a handball court.

- Falling "madly in love" soon after a traumatic breakup seems great for a while: your wildest hopes and fantasies come true! But suddenly the bottom falls out. You discover the new love is *not* that totally sensuous, intelligent, considerate, understanding, sophisticated god/goddess you initially perceived. Only a human, sigh, just like everyone else. Now you have two losses to mourn. Ugh.

Thirty:
Under-indulge in Addictive Activities

- Beware of anything you may be or may become addicted to. *Under* indulgence in the escape mechanisms of society is in order. *Be* with the pain, don't run away from it.

- Alcohol may numb the pain momentarily, but it is a depressant and the eventual effect will be greater depression.

- Drugs (marijuana, ups, downs, all the recreational chemicals) interfere with the natural healing process and should be avoided. A series of momentary "highs" is a poor trade-off for a deepening depression.

- Calorie-junkies beware! You may tend to overeat during this time, allowing "unwanted inches" to creep onto your waistline, causing a lowered self-image, resulting in even more depression. Better visit Weight Watchers instead.

- Smoking more now but enjoying it less?

- If your doctor prescribes medication, a sedative or tranquilizer for example, by all means take it. In that case, the medication is part of your overall recovery program.

Thirty-one:
Pamper Yourself

- If you have a physical injury you are hospitalized, friends bring flowers, relatives bring baskets of fruit, you lie in bed all day, nurses give backrubs—you are pampered.

- If you have an emotional injury, you are expected to show up for work the next morning and be as efficient as ever. You must, in short, deal with a world that simply does not accept the fact that emotional pain *hurts*.

- The solution: pamper yourself.

- The three authors of this volume came up with more suggestions on self-pampering than for any other section of this book. (A revealing insight into our characters.)

- In addition to the suggestions on the following page, do for yourself whatever your parents did to comfort you as a small child.

- Suggestions for pampering yourself:
    —hot baths (no matter how bad you feel, thirty minutes after taking a hot bath you'll feel a lot better)

    —massage (giving/getting, rough and vigorous or slow and sensual.)

    —hot milk and cookies before bed

    —buy yourself something you'd really enjoy

    —treat yourself to your favorite double-dip ice-cream cone (with sprinkles)

    —get a manicure, pedicure, or any other cure

    —take a trip

    —bask in the sun

    —read a good book

    —take time for yourself

    —buy yourself a cashmere anything

    —go to a fine restaurant

    —see a good movie, play, opera, horse race

    —visit an art museum

    —acquiesce to your whims

    —enjoy!

Thirty-two:
Remaining Distraught Is No Proof of Love

- Remaining distraught for a long period of time is no proof that you "really loved." In other words, don't feel "duty-bound" to feel pain any longer than it's actually there.

- Real love is life-supporting. It demands no constant negative response, but instead moves the organism toward joy and greater happiness.

I am missing you
far better than
I ever loved you.

Thirty-three:
Keep a Journal

- You might find keeping a journal or a diary helpful.

- Putting your thoughts and emotions on paper is a good way of getting things out, setting them in order.

- Don't add any "I will make an entry every day or else" rules to your journal keeping. Write when you feel like it, and when you don't, forget it.

(The various authors of this tome have, at one time or another, attempted to keep journals. Only one of us thus far [the compulsive one] has succeeded for more than a single month.)

I write only
until I cry,
which is why
so few poems
this month
have been
completed.

it's just
that

Thirty-four:
There Is a Beauty in Sadness

- There is a certain beauty in sadness, (and here we mean genuine sadness and *not* self-pity).

- We cannot elaborate upon this further (not even the corn-fed poet in our midst dares do that), but thought it was worth mentioning. If you are *enjoying* the beauty of being sad, it's perfectly all right.

Thirty-five:
Heal at Your Own Pace

- Although some people may demand it, don't feel guilty if you fail to immediately "understand" why the loss happened, or instantly "accept" the loss gracefully.

- If you succumb to such pressure and devise a plastic "skin" to cover your wound allowing you to say:
  "That's life"
  "Oh, well"
  "It doesn't matter"
  your phony "acceptances" will be a form of denial which, as was pointed out earlier, interferes with the healing process.

- Remember that healing takes place in three stages. It is your *perfect right* to experience all three, to gain *your* understandings and realizations in your own way, and in your own time.

Thirty-six:
As Healing Continues . . .

• As you continue to heal you will find:
  —your thinking sharper
  —your judgment more reliable
  —your concentration improved
  —your view of the world less self-preoccupied
  —your feelings more alive

• You'll feel stronger and more independent.

a new morning
of a
new life
without you

so?

there will be others.
much finer,
much mine-er.

and until then
there is me.

and because I treated
you
well,
I like me better.

also, the sun rises.

GROWING

and
through
all the tears
and the
sadness
and the
pain
comes the
one thought
that can
make
me internally
smile again:

I
have
loved.

Thirty-seven:
You're Stronger Now

- You've learned that
  - —you can survive
  - —pain eventually lessens
  - —healing does occur

- You've dealt with an experience of loss and have grown from it.

- But don't settle for just surviving and healing. Let growth continue.

the last day of my
loving you is
at hand.

in hand,
a pen, writing one of
the last poems
exclusively yours.

my pain fades,
as my love does,
as autumn did.

winter is too intense
a season to miss
someone in.

the last leaf
fell today.

the first snow
falls tonight.

Thirty-eight:
Forgive the Other Person

- Whenever you can, as soon as you can, forgive the other person.

- To forgive means not just "to pardon." Originally it meant "to return good treatment for ill usage."

- You have been ill-used. As soon as you can return good to the ill-user, without contrivance or compulsion, you are finally free.

Thirty-nine:
Forgive Yourself

- Whenever you can, as soon as you can, forgive yourself.

Forty:
Take Stock of the Good

- Now that the pain is less, understanding can grow.

- You may begin seeing that change and separation are a natural, inevitable and necessary part of life.

- The relationship brought you a great deal of good (that's why you missed it so terribly when it was no longer there). Much of it is still with you. Now is the time to take stock of that good.
    —he taught you to appreciate good food
    —she occasioned your interest in skiing
    —that job taught you a great deal about computers

sifting through the
ashes of our relationship

I find many things
to be grateful for.

I can say "thank you" for
warm mornings,
cold protein drinks,
and all the love you have ever offered
    another.

I can say "thank you"
for being there
willing to be shared.

I can say "thank you" for
the countless poems you were
the inspiration for and the
many changes you were
catalyst to.

but how, in my grasp of
the English Language,
faltering as it is,
can I ever

thank you
    for
Beethoven
    ?

Forty-one:
You Are a Better Person for Having Loved

- You cared. You became involved. You learned to invest yourself. Your interaction permitted loving and caring.

- Even though you lost, you are a better person for having loved.

You were the best of loves,
you were the worst of loves . . .

and you left behind several
unintended gifts:

through you I re-examined my
need (uh, desire?) for one significant
other to share my life-space with.

you commanded in me an unwilling
re-evaluation of self, behavior patterns,
relationshipping, & a corresponding
change in attitudes; i.e.: growth.

I'm nicer to people.

I'm more in touch with my feelings,
the things and persons around me, life.

And, of course, a scattering of poems
(the best of poems, the worst of poems)
that never would have been without
your disruptions.

  Thanks.

Forty-two:
Changes

- Prepare to make an adjustment . . . maybe even two or three.

- A new chapter in your life has begun (and is by now well under way).

- Know that you will have to make the changes this new chapter requires.

- Now might be a good time to start experimenting with new life styles, new ways of filling the day-to-day needs that are still unattended.

- It will take courage, but at the same time it's exciting.

- This might even turn out to be fun!

the need you
grew
still remains.

but less and less
you seem the way
to fill that need.

I am.

Forty-three:
Praise Yourself for the Courage to Relate

- You are a richer, deeper, wiser person for having invested in a relationship, even if that relationship didn't quite work out.

- *Praise yourself* for the courage to relate.

- Would we dare quote something as clichéd and corny as "It is far, far better to have loved and lost than never to have loved at all"? Of course we wouldn't.

Forty-four:
Start Anew

- Be open.

- Be open to new people, places, ideas, experiences.

- It's time to move far beyond the "I'll never love again—love only brings pain" attitude.

- Do your best to
    —remain trusting
    —maintain a lively curiosity
    —continue developing your willingness to learn

- Visit new places.

- Now's the time to
    —redecorate (or at least clean) your apartment
    —buy (or make) some new clothes
    —go back to school
    —learn—whatever it is you've always wanted to know.

Forty-five:
Invite New People into Your Life

- Now is the time to make new friends, associates, colleagues.

- Attend meetings, concerts, plays, socials—any public gathering of kindred souls. (Don't be afraid to go alone.)

- Meet your neighbors.

- Don't be afraid to introduce yourself to anyone—even a total stranger.

- When making new acquaintances ask questions that require more than a "yes" or "no" answer.

- Use "how" and "why" questions rather than only "what" or "who."

- Offer to drive people home or invite them out for a cup of coffee.

- Carry some paper and a pen to collect and share phone numbers.

Someday we are going to be lovers.
Maybe married.
At the very least, an affair.

What's your name?

Forty-six:
Develop New Interests . . .

- Now's the time to develop new interests.

- Archery's always held some fascination? How about water polo? And just about everyone's learning tennis these days.

- Is it time to get that personal computer?

- A new language? Brush up on an old language? (English perhaps?) How about a course in bookkeeping—or bee keeping?

- Gardening? Sewing? Canning? Auto maintenance? Garment weaving? Gourmet cooking? Metal shop?

- Read a book. Take a class. Learn—and above all *do*—something new.

Forty-seven:
. . . But Don't Forget the Old Interests

• Don't forget about the old interests and activities you've let lapse.

• Re-discover the ones that gave you a special sense of achievement, excitement, joy.

• In choosing new and old interests, be sure to intersperse those activities which require people and those which you do best alone.

Forty-eight:
Groups

* Perhaps you feel shy or simply don't want to make new contacts on your own. If so, groups may be the answer.

* There are literally hundreds of groups you can join. Check the Yellow Pages under "Clubs," "Associations," "Fellowships," etc. You can join a group to learn something, to travel, to meet people, to celebrate common interests—many possibilities.

* Church sponsored groups are readily available.

* There are many groups that cater especially to the newly-single-again individual. They include:
    —Parents Without Partners
    —The Singletons
    —Singles Dating Club
    —Over-30 Club

* The Toastmaster's Club helps develop speaking skills that may be helpful in addressing yourself to others.

* Adult Education Classes, "Y" groups, and programs sponsored by The American Youth Hostels offer opportunities not only for learning new skills, but for meeting others in a comparatively protected environment.

Forty-nine:
Self-improvement, Anyone?

- By now it may be time to change (one at a time) something about yourself that you'd like to change.
    - —go on a diet
    - —stop smoking
    - —stop drinking

Seek professional help if necessary, and/or join a recognized group (AA, Weight Watchers, etc.). Be gentle with yourself, but set a realistic goal and then achieve it.

- At the same time, accentuate your positives. Be even more
    - —tolerant
    - —trusting/trustworthy
    - —helpful
    - —giving
    - —concerned
    - —loving
    - —yourself

- Melba and Peter highly recommend a workshop called Insight I: The Awakening Heart Seminar. It is given all over the country. For more information, please call 800-777-7750.

Fifty:
Do Something for Someone Else

- If you begin feeling sorry for yourself (not genuine sorrow, but the "poor put-upon me" variety) the best way to deal with this is to do something for someone else.

  —drive someone to the grocery store
  —tune a friend's car
  —volunteer to take calls at the local suicide prevention service, rap line, hot line, or similar service
  —become a "Big Brother" or "Big Sister"
  —visit someone in a hospital—anyone
  —wash windows or do housework for an older person
  —read to the blind
  —talk to the lonely
  —listen to the ignored

- Giving is the greatest joy.

In being loved
I am filled full.

In loving
I am fulfilled.

the greatest gift
is to fill a need
unnoticed

Fifty-one:
The Past

- Remember: the healing process continues even while you're growing.

- Memories may come drifting back one Sunday morning or when "our song" is played on the radio.

- Expect this. It doesn't mean you're sinking back into depression, it's just the ebb and flow of healing and growing.

- Be with the feeling. Know that it soon will pass.

I know our
time together
is no more.

then why do
words
come to mind
that call you
back?

Why do I plan
lifetimes
that include
you?

Why do I
torture
myself
with love
I never felt
while you were
here?

Fifty-two:
Solitude

• You can now be comfortably alone with yourself again.

• In addition to moving outward into the world, explore and enjoy your personal world of solitude.

• Solitary pursuits can be
  —delight-filled
  —restful
  —exciting
  —in joy able
  —a prelude to creative activities
  —fun

• Enjoying yourself alone is a prerequisite to genuinely enjoying others.

unpremeditated passion.
sadness so pure.
complete smile.
clean pain.
joy untainted.

each moment
fully felt—

uncontaminated
by the one
only a moment before.

Fifty-three:
Creativity

- What do you do that is creative? Write? Sing? Dance? Act? Bake cherry pies? Give massages?

- Well, whatever it is or they are, **DO!**

- You'll find yourself once again remarkably in touch with your creative energy. Do something with it.

For example, did you know that you are a poet? Prove it to yourself. Sit down with pencil and paper. (Pen and paper will do.) Find out what you're feeling, find a thought or group of words that fits that feeling, and write them down.

Now, instead of writing the words this way,

write
them
this way.

Put words that you want to
stand
out
on separate lines.
Forget
every
thing
"they" taught you about
poetry
in
school.

Do this three or four times. Keep it up. You'll get a poem. Honest.

Rule 1: line for line, poetry need not rhyme
Rule 2: honest clear expression of a fully felt experience
is what poetry is all about

Fifty-four:
Appreciation

- As you grow you will begin to regain your sense of appreciation, of awe. The sense of childlike wonder, which was lost to you for a while, will return.

- Enjoy it.

- Sunsets and children laughing. City streets and country roads. The wonder of "this time called life."

the cosmic dance
to celestial melodies

free form within
patterns of precise
limitations.

The painting I know
so well. The canvas
I want to learn.

and perhaps
someday,
the artist.

Fifty-five:
Growth

- Having weathered a crisis, expect to discover
  —a stronger you
  —a different you
  —a more evolved you

- You're changing and growing into a
  —happier you
  —more joyful you
  —an independent you

I'm not quite
as certain of
my uncertainties.

I am beginning to
doubt my doubts.

And I'm having
second thoughts
about my
second thoughts.

I appreciate solitude.
I romanticize it sometimes.

Some growth has taken place.
I haven't taken time to
notice.

Fifty-six:
Freedom to Choose

• Enjoy your freedom.

• You're in control now.

• Make the most of the ability to choose
  —where
  —what
  —how
  —when
  —who

• You can make (and make well) the necessary decisions to
  —sort
  —clean
  —re-arrange
  —discard
  —acquire

• You are bringing order into your world again. You can choose the world you want to have around you.

The world is good.

I feel whole & directed.

Touch my Joy with me.

I cannot keep
my smiles
in single file.

Fifty-seven:
Celebrate Your Survival

- Throw a Survival Celebration party.

- Invite everyone who helped in your survival, healing and growth. Ask each one of them to bring a friend (a great way to meet new people).

- If a party is not your style, be sure to acknowledge the help and support you received from others. Send out thank you notes or flowers or gifts or whatever you deem appropriate.

- Remember the value of the help you received when you come across others in need.

I am worthy.

I am worthy of my life and
all the good that is in it.

I am worthy of
my friends and their friendship.

I am worthy of spacious skies, amber waves
of grain, and purple mountain majesties
above the fruited plain. (I am worthy, too,
of the fruited plain.)

I am worthy of a degree of happiness
that could only be referred to as
"sinful" in less enlightened times.

I am worthy of creativity,
sensitivity and appreciation.

I am worthy of peace of mind, peace on Earth,
peace in the valley, and a piece of the action.

I am worthy of God's presence in my life.

I am worthy
            of your love.

Fifty-eight:
A Pat on the Back for a Job Well Done

- You've been through losing, surviving, healing and growing.

- It's time now for celebrating.

CONGRATULATIONS!

I loved,
which was purgatory.

I lost,
which was hell.

and I survived.
Heaven!

MELBA COLGROVE has earned degrees in literature, foreign trade, special education, counseling and organizational psychology. She received her Ph.D. in 1966 from the University of Michigan, having written her doctoral dissertation on creative problem solving.

HAROLD H. BLOOMFIELD, M.D., is a practising psychiatrist and a world renowned and much sought-after speaker and seminar leader. He has made hundreds of major presentations for corporations, universities and the general public. Bestselling books he has authored or co-authored include: HOW TO SURVIVE THE LOSS OF A LOVE, MAKING PEACE WITH YOUR PARENTS, INNER JOY, TM: DISCOVERING INNER ENERGY AND OVERCOMING STRESS, THE HOLISTIC WAY TO HEALTH AND HAPPINESS, HOW TO ENJOY THE LOVE OF YOUR LIFE and THE ACHILLES SYNDROME: TRANSFORMING YOUR WEAKNESSES INTO STRENGTHS. Dr. Bloomfield completed his psychiatric training at Yale University School of Medicine and is a member of the American Psychiatric Association. He is the director of psychiatry, psychotherapy and family counseling at the North County Holistic Health Center in Del Mar, California.

PETER McWILLIAMS published his first book of poetry at the tender age of seventeen. He now has nine volumes in print, which have sold over three million copies. A book of verse and advice, published in 1971, SURVIVING THE LOSS OF A LOVE became the inspiration for HOW TO SURVIVE THE LOSS OF A LOVE. Peter co-authored THE TM BOOK, which became a number-one bestseller on the *New York Times* trade paperback list. He is also the author of THE PERSONAL COMPUTER BOOK, PERSONAL COMPUTERS AND THE DISABLED and THE WORD PROCESSING BOOK. His most recent book (co-authored with John-Roger) is YOU CAN'T AFFORD THE LUXURY OF A NEGATIVE THOUGHT: A BOOK FOR PEOPLE WITH ANY LIFE-THREATENING ILLNESS—INCLUDING LIFE.